FIRST LADIES OF
USA

FIRST LADIES OF
USA

Part 2

Marshella Marshall

FIRST LADIES OF USA
PART 2

iUniverse books may be ordered through booksellers or by contacting:

iUniverse
1663 Liberty Drive
Bloomington, IN 47403
www.iuniverse.com
1-800-Authors (1-800-288-4677)

ISBN: 978-1-5320-7625-1 (sc)
ISBN: 978-1-5320-7626-8 (e)

Library of Congress Control Number: 2019906870

Print information available on the last page.

iUniverse rev. date: 05/31/2019

Frances Folsom Cleveland
July 21, 1864 – October 29, 1947

22nd President Wife

Frances Folsom Cleveland
Born: July 21, 1864 Buffalo, New York
Died: October 27, 1947, Baltimore, Maryland
Mother: Emma Harmon Folsom
Father: Oscar Folsom
First Marriage: February 10, 1913 Thomas J Preston (1870-1955)
Children: Ruth Cleveland (1891-1904) Ester Cleveland (1893-1980) Marion Cleveland (1895-1977) Richard Folsom Cleveland (1897-1974) Francis Grove Cleveland (1903-95)

Caroline Harrison
October 1, 1832 – October 25, 1892

23rd President Wife

Carolina Lavina Scott Harrison
Born: October 1, 1822 Oxford, Ohio
Died: October 25, 1892 Washington, DC
Mother: Mary Potts Neal Scott
Father: John Witherspoon Scott
First Marriage: October 20, 1853 to Benjamin Harrison (1833-1901)
Children: Russel Lord 'Russel Benjamin' (1854-1963) Mary 'Mamie' Scott (1858-1930) unnamed stillborn child (1861)

Ida Saxton McKinley
June 8, 1847 – May 26, 1907

24th President Wife

Ida Saxton Mckinley
Born: June 8, 1947 Canton, Ohio
Died: May 16, 1907 Canton, Ohio
Mother: Katherine DeWalt Saxton
Father: James A. Saxton
First Marriage: January 25, 1871 to William McKinley, Jr. (1843-1901)
Children: Katherine (1871-75) Ida (1873)

Ediith Roosevelt
August 6, 1861 – September 30, 1948

25th President Wife

Edith Kermit Carow Roosevelt
Born: August 6, 1861 Norwich, Connecticut
Died: September 30, 1948 Oyster Bay, New York
Mother: Gertrude Tyler
Father: Charles Carow
First Marriage: December 2, 1886 to Theodore Roosevelt
Children: Theodore, Jr. (1887-1944) Kermit (1889-1943)
Ethel Carow (1891-1977) Archibald Bulloch (1894-1979)
Quentin (1897-1918) Stepdaughter Alice Lee Roosevelt
Longworth (1884-1980)

Helen Herron Taft
June 2, 1861 – May 22, 1943

26th President Wife

Helen Herron Taft
Born: June 2, 1861 Cincinnati, Ohio
Died: May 22, 1943 Washington DC
Mother: Harriet Collins Herron
Father: John Williamson
First Marriage: June 19, 1886 to William Howard Taft (1857)
Children: Robert Alphonso (1889-1953) Helen Herron (1891-1987) Charles Phelps (1897-1983)

Ellen Axson Wilson
May 15, 1860 – August 6, 1914

27th President Wife

Edith Bolling Galt Wilson
Born: October 15, 1872 Wytheville, Virginia
Died: December 28, 1961 Washington DC
Mother: Sallie White Bolling
Father: William Holcomber Bolling
First Marriage: April 30, 1896 to Norman Galt (1862-1908)
Remarried December 18, 1915 Thomas Woodrow Wilson (1856-1924)
Children: None

Florence Harding
August 15, 1860 – November 21, 1924

28th President Wife

Florence Mabel King De Wolfe Harding
Born: August 15, 1860 Marion, Ohio
Died: November 21, 1924 Marion, Ohio
Mother: Louise Mabel Bouton King
Father: Amos Hall King
First Marriage: March 1880 Henry Athenton De Wolfe, remarried July 8, 1891 Warren G. Harding (1865-1923)
Children: Marshal Eugene De Wolfe

Grace Coolidge
January 3, 1879 – July 8, 1957

29th President Wife

Grace Anna Goodhue Coolridge
Born: January 3, 1879 Burlington, Vermont
Died: July 8, 1957 Northhampton, Massachusetts
Mother: Lemira Barrett Goodhue
Father: Andrew Issacher
First Marriage: October 4, 1905 to Calvin Coolridge
Children: John (1906-2000) Calvin Jr. (1908-24)

Lou Henry Hoover
March 29, 1874 – January 7, 1944

30th President Wife

Louise Henry Hoover
Born: March 29, 1874 Waterloo, Iowa
Died: January 7, 1944 New York, New York
Mother: Florence Ida Ward Henry
Father: Charles Delano Henry
First Marriage: February 10, 1899 to Herbert Hoover (1874-1964)
Children: Herbert Charles (1903-69) Allan Henry (1907-93)

Eleanor Roosevelt
October 11, 1884 – November 7, 1962

31st President Wife

Anna Eleanor Roosevelt
Born: October 11, 1884 New York, New York
Died: November 7, 1962 Hyde Park, New York
Mother: Anna Rebecca Hall Roosevelt
Father: Elliot Roosevelt
First Marriage: March 17, 1905 Franklin Delano Roosevelt (1882-1945)
Children: Anna Eleanor (1906-75) James (1907-91) Franklin Delano, Jr. (1909) Elliot Delano (1901-90) Franklin Delano Jr. (1914-88) John Spinal (1916-81)

Bess Truman
February 13, 1885 – October 18, 1982

32nd President Wife

Elizabeth Virginia Wallace Truman
Born: February 13, 1885 Independence, Missouri
Died: October 18, 1982 Independence, Missouri
Mother: Margaret Gates Wallace
Father: David Willock Wallace
First Marriage: June 28, 1919 Henry Truman (1884-1972)
Children: Mary Margaret (1924-2008)

Mamie Eisenhower
November 14, 1896 – November 1, 1979

33rd President Wife

Mary Geneva Doud Eisenhower
Born: November 14, 1896 Boone, Iowa
Died: November 1, 1979 Washington DC
Mother: Elivera Mathilda Carlson Doud
Father: John Sheldon Duod
First Marriage: July 1,1916 to Dwight David Eisenhower
Children: Doud Dwight (1917-21) John Sheldon Doud (1922-??)

Jacqueline Kennedy
July 28, 1929 – May 19, 1994

34ᵗʰ President Wife

Jacqueline Lee Bouvier Kennedy
Born: July 28, 1929 Southampton, New York
Died: May 19, 1994 New York, New York]
Mother: Janet Norton Lee Bouvier (Auchincloss)
Father: John Vernon Bouvier III
First Marriage: September 12, 1953 to John Fitzgerald Kennedy (1917-63), remarried October 20, 1968 to Aristotle Onassis (1906-75)
Children: Caroline Bouvier (1957-??) John Fitzgerald Jr. (1960-99) Patrick Bouvier (1963-63)

Lady Bird Johnson
December 22, 1912 – July 11, 2007

35th President Wife

Claudia Alta Taylor Johnson
Nickname: Lady Bird Johnson
Born: December 22, 1912 Karnack, Texas
Died: July 11, 2007 Austin, Texas
Mother: Minnie Lee Pattillo Taylor
Father: Thomas Jefferson Taylor
First Marriage: November 17, 1934 to Lyndon Baines Johnson (1905-73)
Children: Lynda Bird (1944-??) Lucy Baines (1947-??)

Pat Nixon
March 16, 1912 – June 22, 1993

36th President Wife

Thelma Catherine Ryan Nixon
Nickname: Pat Nixon
Born: March 16, 1912 Ely, Nevada
Died: June 22, 1993 Yorba Linda, California
Mother: Katherine Halberstaat Bender Ryan
Father: William Ryan
First Marriage: June 21, 1940 Richard Milhous Nixon (1913-94)
Children: Patrici (1946-?) Julie (1948-?)

Betty Ford
April 8, 1918 – July 8, 2011

37th President Wife

Elizabeth Ann Bloomer Warren Ford
Nickname: Betty Ford
Born: April 8, 1918 Chicago, Illinois
Died: July 8, 2011 Rancho Mirage California
Mother: Hortense Neahr Bloomer
Father: William Stephenson Bloomer
First Marriage: William G. Warren in 1942
Remarried October 15, 1948 Gerald R. Ford (1913-2006)
Children: Michael Gerald (1950-?) John Gardener (1952-?)
Steven Meigs (1956-?) Susan Elizabeth (1957-?)

Eleanor Rosalynn Smith
Born August 18, 1927

38th Wife President

Eleanor Rosalynn Smith Carter
Nickname: Rosalynn Carter
Born: August 18, 1927 Botsford, Georgia
Died: None
Mother: France Allethra Murray Smith
Father: Wilburn Edgar Smith
First Marriage: James Earl Carter (1924-?)
Children: John William 'Jack' (1947-?) James Earl 'Chip' (1950-?) Donnel Jeffrey (1952-?) Amy Lynn (1967-?)

Nancy Regan
July 6, 1921 – March 6, 2016

39th President Wife

Anne Drance Robbins
Nickname: Nancy Raegan
Born: July 6, 1921 New York, New York
Died: None
Mother: Edith Luckett Robbins
Father: Kenneth Seymour
First Marriage: March 4, 1952 Ronald Raegan (1911-2004)
Children: Patricia Ann (1952-?) Ronald Prescot (1958-?) step-daughter Maureen Elizabeth (1941-2001) step-son Michael Edward(1945-?)

Barbara Bush
Born June 8, 1925

40th President Wife

Barbara Pierce Bush
Born: June 8, 1925 New York, New York
Died: None
Mother: Pauline Robinson Pierce
Father: Marvin Pierce
First Marriage: January 6, 1945 George Herbert Walker Bush
Children: George Walker (1946-?) Robin (1949-1953) Jonh
Ellis 'Jeb'(1953-?) Neil Mallon (1955-?) Marvin Peirce (1956-
?) Dorothy Walker (1959-?)

Hillary Clinton
Born October 26, 1947

41st President Wife

Hillary Dianne Rodham Clinton
Nickname: Hillary Clinton
Born: October 26, 1947, Chicago, Illinois
Died: None
Mother: Dorothy Howell Rodham
Father: Hugh Ellsworth
First Marriage: October 11, 1975 to William Jefferson Clinton
(1946-?)
Children: Chelsea Victoria (1980-present)

Laura Bush
Born November 4, 1946

42nd President Wife

Laura Welch Bush
Born: November 4,1946 Midland, Texas
Died: None
Mother: Jenna Hawkins Welch
Father: Harold Bruce Welch
First Marriage: November 5, 1977 to George Walker Bush
(1946-?)
Children: Barbara Pierce (1981-?) Jenna Welch (1981-?)

Michelle Obama
Born January 17, 1964

43rd President Wife

Michelle LaVaughn Robinson Obama
Born: January 17, 1964 Chicago, Illinois
Mother: Marian Shield Robinson
Father: Fraser Robinson
First Marriage: October 18, 1992 Barack Hussein Obama Jr.
(1961-?)
Children: Malia Ann (1998-?) Natasha

Printed in the United States
By Bookmasters